Binoculars

Robin Koontz

Educational Media

rourkeeducationalmedia.com

Scan for Related Titles
and Teacher Resources

Teaching Focus:

Concepts of Print: Ending Punctuation- Have students locate the ending punctuation for sentences in the book. Count how many times a period, question mark, or exclamation point is used. Which one is used the most? What is the purpose for each ending punctuation mark? Practice reading these sentences with appropriate expression.

Before Reading:

Building Academic Vocabulary and Background Knowledge

Before reading a book, it is important to set the stage for your child or student by using pre-reading strategies. This will help them develop their vocabulary, increase their reading comprehension, and make connections across the curriculum.

1. *Read the title and look at the cover. Let's make predictions about what this book will be about.*
2. *Take a picture walk by talking about the pictures/photographs in the book. Implant the vocabulary as you take the picture walk. Be sure to talk about the text features such as headings, Table of Contents, glossary, bolded words, captions, charts/ diagrams, or Index.*
3. Have students read the first page of text with you then have students read the remaining text.
4. *Strategy Talk – use to assist students while reading.*
    - *Get your mouth ready*
    - *Look at the picture*
    - *Think…does it make sense*
    - *Think…does it look right*
    - *Think…does it sound right*
    - *Chunk it – by looking for a part you know*
5. *Read it again.*
6. *After reading the book complete the activities below.*

Content Area Vocabulary
Use glossary words in a sentence.

convex
lenses
magnify
objective lenses
prisms
view

After Reading:

Comprehension and Extension Activity

After reading the book, work on the following questions with your child or students in order to check their level of reading comprehension and content mastery.

1. *What does convex mean? (Summarize)*
2. *Why are there two lenses in binoculars? (Asking questions)*
3. *Why would people use binoculars? (Text to self connection)*
4. *What does magnify mean? (Summarize)*

Extension Activity

Let's see how your eyes compare to binoculars! Find an object the size of a medium box. Place the object 10 feet (3.05 m) away from you. Can you see it clearly? Now look at that object using binoculars. How does it look? Now move the object 20 feet (6.1 m) away from you. Record your observations using binoculars and using your eyes. Continue to move the object every 10 feet (3.05 m) and record your observations. When did your eyes stop seeing the object clearly? How far could you see the object when you used binoculars?

Table of Contents

What Are Binoculars?

Binoculars help us see things that are far away.

They make things appear closer than they really are!

Binoculars are like two telescopes that are put together.

telescope

We use both eyes to look through binocular **lenses.**

binoculars

People also use binoculars to **view** the night sky.

Some people use binoculars to spy on other people!

The first binoculars were used to watch plays.

Close-up World

How do binoculars make things look closer and bigger?

Binoculars use special lenses to **magnify** things, making them look bigger.

without binoculars

with binoculars

13

Binoculars have two sets of **convex** lenses.

lenses

Convex means that the sides are thinner than the middle of the glass.

thin

thick

thin

The lenses that point at the object are called the **objective lenses.**

Light passes through the objective lenses. They show an image through the eyepiece lenses.

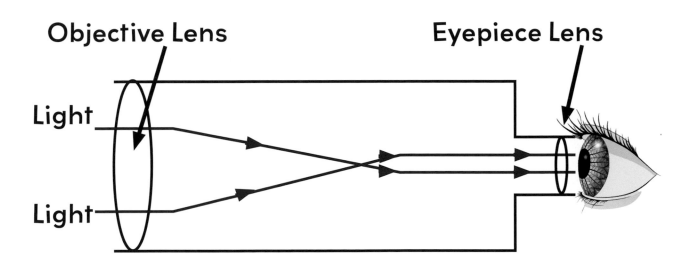

Objective Lens

Eyepiece Lens

Light

Light

Hold the small lenses to your eyes.

These lenses magnify the image.

Some binoculars can magnify to different sizes. They are called zoom binoculars.

Flipping It Over

When light goes through a lens, it flips the image upside down!

But binoculars have more glass shapes inside called **prisms.** Prisms flip the image so that it looks right-side up.

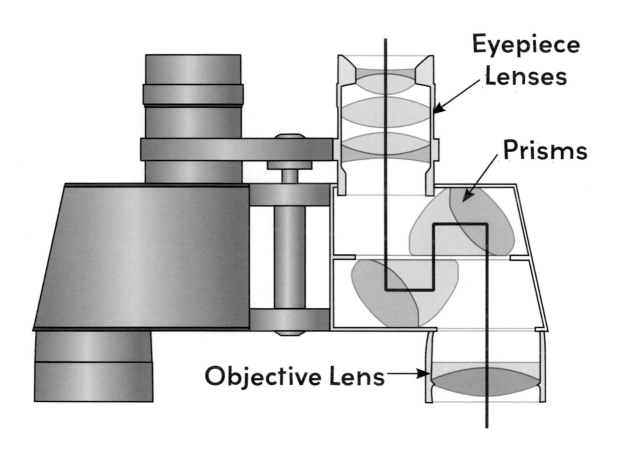

Eyepiece Lenses

Prisms

Objective Lens

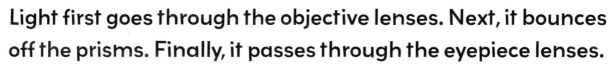

Light first goes through the objective lenses. Next, it bounces off the prisms. Finally, it passes through the eyepiece lenses.

Binoculars give us a close-up view of our world!

Binoculars are great for sightseeing!

Photo Glossary

 **convex** (KON-veks): Curved outward, like the outer side of a ball.

 **lenses** (linz-iz): Pieces of curved glass or plastic in eyeglasses, cameras, and binoculars.

 **magnify** (MAG-nuh-fye): To make something appear larger.

 **objective lenses** (uhb-JEK-tiv linz-iz): The lenses nearest to the object being viewed.

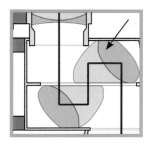 **prisms** (PRIZ-uhms): Clear glass or plastic shapes that bend light.

 **view** (VYOO): To look at something.

Index

Websites to Visit

www.birdwatching.com/optics/how_binoculars_work.html

www.whatbird.com/game/game.aspx

www.birdsource.org/gbbc/kids

About the Author

Robin Koontz is an author and illustrator of a wide variety of books and articles for children and young adults. She uses binoculars to view the Coast Range of western Oregon, where she lives with her husband.

Meet The Author!
www.meetREMauthors.com

© 2015 Rourke Educational Media

www.rourkeeducationalmedia.com

PHOTO CREDITS: Cover © Evgeny Karandaev; title page, page 8, 16 © Yuri_Arcurs; page 4, 22 © Saturated; page 5 © Stephanie Howard, zanskar; page 6, 23 © Roman_Gorielov; page 7, 23 © Mandy Godbehear; page 9 © nojustice; page 10 © Yuriy Mazur; page 11 © John Pavel; page 12 © Sam74100; page 13 © Jeff Goulden; page 14 © Dragon Images; page 15 © VERSUSstudio; page 17 © Diana Glushkova; page 18, 22 © Nanette Greve, Herbert Kratky; page 19 © Michha; page 20, 23 Antivied/Wikipedia; page 21 © magnez2, xyno, oytun karadayi; page

Edited by: Jill Sherman

Cover design by: Nicola Stratford, www.nicolastratford.com

Interior design by: Jen Thomas

Library of Congress PCN Data

Binoculars / Robin Koontz
(How It Works)
ISBN (hard cover)(alk. paper) 978-1-62717-640-8
ISBN (soft cover) 978-1-62717-762-7
ISBN (e-Book) 978-1-62717-882-2
Library of Congress Control Number: 2014934207

Printed in the United States of America, North Mankato, Minnesota

Also Available as:

ROURKE'S
e-Books